Wonderfully and Purposely Made

I Am Enough

A Journal All About Me

Wonderfully and Purposely Made

I Am Enough

A Journal All About Me

Cheryl B. Evans

Published by Cheryl B. Evans - Ontario, Canada

www.writtenbymom.ca

You are encouraged to have fun with your journal.
Write, draw and create your own magic within its pages.

First Published in 2018
Paperback ISBN: 978-0-9951807-8-9 (Light Bulb Cover)
First Edition

Library and Archives Canada Cataloguing in Publication
Printed in the United States of America

Other books by Cheryl B. Evans include:
I Promised Not to Tell: Raising a transgender child
What Does God Think? Transgender People and The Bible.
My Parenting Journey with an LGBTQ+ Child: A Journal
My Parenting Journey with a Transgender Child: A Journal

I am wonderfully
and purposely
made – and
I am enough!

Wonderfully and Purposely Made

I Am Enough

A Journal All About Me

This journal was created to help celebrate you! So, go ahead - splash your style, charisma, and individuality across the pages, and don't forget to share a little of your heart and soul along the way.

The Date I started this journal: / /

Doodle, write, and create magic within these pages to your heart's content.

Chapter

One

Who I Am

Wonderfully and Purposely Made
I Am Enough
A Journal All About Me

My name is:

_____

My pronouns are:

_____

There is no right or wrong way to be transgender. We are all human in our own way, and I am no exception. My experiences are as unique and individual as I am, but here's what being transgender means to me...

_____

_____

_____

_____

_____

_____

_____

_____

_____

_____

I knew I was transgender when...

_____

_____

_____

_____

_____

_____

Things I remember about that day or time are...

_____

_____

_____

_____

_____

_____

_____

_____

_____

I remember feeling...

_____

_____

_____

_____

_____

The person I first shared my truth with was:

_____

Their reaction to my truth was…

_____

_____

_____

_____

_____

_____

Looking back, I can honestly say…

_____

_____

_____

_____

_____

I am wonderfully
and purposely made.

Some of the ways I've grown through my unique experiences are…

My purpose is not to be like everyone else.
My purpose is to be ME.

I have some awesome qualities. Here are just a few:

My favorite quality is:

I am my
own
free spirit.

Stealth or Activist
or somewhere in the middle?

How do I see myself living my transgender life? Am I living stealthily, as an activist, or am I somewhere in the middle?

Today, I am living…

_____

_____

_____

_____

_____

_____

How might this look for me down the road? Will the way I live today change? If so, what might influence that change?

_____

_____

_____

_____

_____

_____

Not Everyone Gets Me,

And That is OK!

I'm me, and I'm the only one that will ever fully understand the path I'm walking. There are some ignorant people out there, and their opinion of me is none of my business.

Just for fun, here's what I really want to tell those people who don't understand me:

My kind and patient version...

_____

_____

_____

_____

_____

_____

_____

_____

_____

I am all I need to be!

Now, my brutally honest, in-your-face version...

That felt good!

Why does gender matter? Why do I believe different places around the world
vary so much in their acceptance of gender variant people?

My Gender, My Way
The things I love about my gender…

Write about the first time I met
another transgender person.

If that hasn't happened yet, how would I imagine the experience to be?

Quotes I Love:

Fill this page with quotes you love.

Here's a letter to my future self.
(Don't forget to date it. ☺)

Chapter
Two

Gratitude

Design a Gratitude Banner

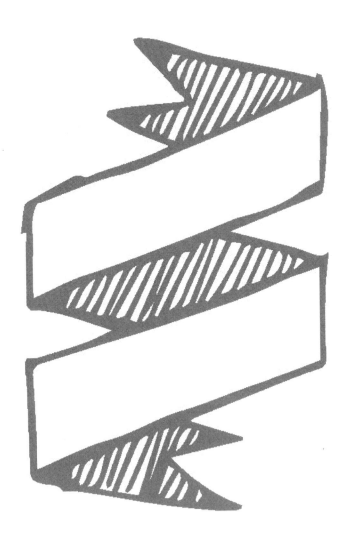

Gratitude

The feeling of being grateful and giving thanks for what we already have is one of the most powerful practices we can use for a positive and joyous life.

Gratitude Challenge: Every day, for the next 100 days, write something I am grateful for.

1. _____

2. _____

3. _____

4. _____

5. _____

6. _____

7. _____

8. _____

9. _____

10. _____

11. _____

12. _____

13. _____

14. _____

15. _____

16. _____

17. _____

18. _____

19. _____

20. _____

21. _____

22. _____

23. _____

24. _____

25. _____

26. _____

27. _____

28. _____

29. _____

30. _____

31. _____

32. _____

33. _____

34. _____

35. _____

36. _____

37. _____

38. _____

39. _____

40. _____

41. _____

42. _____

43. _____

44. _____

45. _____

46. _____

47. _____

48. _____
49. _____
50. _____
51. _____
52. _____
53. _____
54. _____
55. _____
56. _____
57. _____
58. _____
59. _____
60. _____
61. _____
62. _____
63. _____
64. _____
65. _____
66. _____
67. _____
68. _____
69. _____
70. _____
71. _____
72. _____
73. _____
74. _____
75. _____

76. _____

77. _____

78. _____

79. _____

80. _____

81. _____

82. _____

83. _____

84. _____

85. _____

86. _____

87. _____

88. _____

89. _____

90. _____

91. _____

92. _____

93. _____

94. _____

95. _____

96. _____

97. _____

98. _____

99. _____

100. _____

Whenever I need to add a little thankfulness to my day,
this list will serve as a reminder that there is ALWAYS
someone, someplace, or something to be grateful for.

The People I am Grateful For and Why...

I am truly grateful when others see me for my authentic self.

The Places I am Grateful For and Why...

The Things I am Grateful For and Why...

A thank you note to someone I owe a debt of gratitude to:

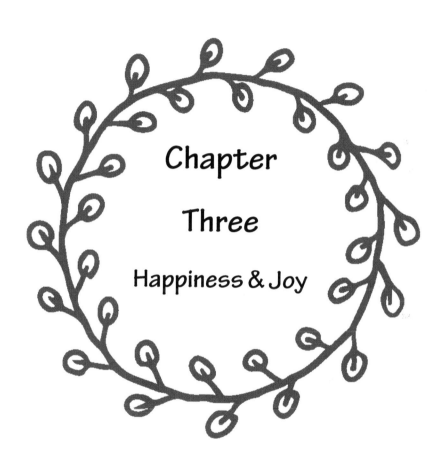

Chapter

Three

Happiness & Joy

You can't buy happiness,
but you can buy cupcakes, and
it's kind of the same thing. ☺

My favourite kind of cupcake:

Happiness ☺

These are some of the things that make me happy:

_____

_____

_____

_____

_____

_____

_____

_____

_____

_____

_____

_____

_____

My happy 'peeps' are those who make me smile. They lift me up and make me laugh. They are the deliverers of my sunshine. They are… (Write their names, draw their pictures, or paste their photos below).

Write, draw or paste a picture on this page about a place that brings me happiness.

What things do I enjoy most? It's time to let my creativity flow onto this page.

Here's a time when music brought me joy
and what that experience meant to me:

_____

_____

_____

_____

_____

_____

_____

_____

_____

_____

_____

Music is food for the soul!

Inspiration from my favourite songs:

My Greatest Joy

When or where do I experience my greatest joy?
Is it when I am alone in nature? Listening to music?
Singing in the shower? Here are my experiences:

Some of my thoughts on a new skill or hobby that I would like to pursue just for the joy of it:

Where could I go to find out more about that?

My innate gender identity is one to be celebrated, protected, and cherished. A transgender life with joy comes in knowing I am wonderfully and purposely made.

What, if anything, is blocking my joy?

_____

_____

_____

_____

_____

_____

_____

_____

_____

_____

_____

_____

_____

_____

How can I celebrate my uniqueness and find more joy?

Who do I know who is always joyous? What lessons could I learn from looking at their life?

_____

_____

_____

_____

_____

_____

_____

_____

_____

_____

_____

_____

_____

_____

_____

_____

_____

_____

(It is important to acknowledge that joyous people have difficult times too, even if I am unaware of them.)

I choose to
be happy.
I choose
to feel joy.

Life is Richer with Books

This is a list of some of the best books I have enjoyed and some of the books I want to read.

Books I Enjoyed:

_____

_____

_____

_____

_____

_____

_____

_____

Books I Want to Read:

_____

_____

_____

_____

_____

_____

If my life were a book, the title would be:

_____

This is the first paragraph of my story...

_____

_____

_____

_____

_____

_____

_____

_____

_____

_____

_____

_____

_____

_____

_____

_____

_____

_____

_____

I decide what this life will bring me - will it be joy or sorrow? Will I harness the power within and decide to be fabulous, or will I doubt, fear, and limit the wonderful being I am?

These are some ways I can elevate my joy...

_____

_____

_____

_____

_____

_____

_____

_____

_____

_____

What influences do I have on my life that makes elevating my joy challenging?

_____

_____

_____

_____

_____

_____

_____

_____

It was the funniest thing…..

This page is dedicated to remembering my crazy moments and silly mishaps - those times that bring a smile to my face whenever I recall them.

My Happiest Day

When was it? What happened? Who was there?

Laughter is Food for the Soul.

These are things I can do today to laugh more:

_____

_____

_____

_____

_____

_____

_____

_____

_____

_____

_____

_____

A joke or a memory that always makes me laugh:

_____

_____

_____

_____

Chapter

Four

Love

Love

Love flows through my heart,
out to others, and back to me.

One of the most important things to know about love is that it starts with me. Before I can show love to others, I must first have love for myself. Self-love is something we should all strive for, but for some, it is not an easy task. What can I do to show myself more love?

_____

_____

_____

_____

_____

_____

_____

_____

_____

_____

_____

_____

_____

_____

_____

_____

_____

What negative things do I think or say about myself that I know I should change?

_____

_____

_____

_____

_____

_____

_____

_____

_____

_____

_____

_____

_____

_____

• ♥ • • ♥ • • ♥ • • ♥ • • ♥ • • ♥ •

How I speak to myself about myself
is more important than any words
anyone else can ever say to me.

What can I begin telling myself today that can help me to love myself more?

What does love mean to me?

♡

_____

_____

_____

_____

_____

How can I show more love to others?

♡

_____

_____

_____

_____

How can others show me more love?

♡

_____

_____

_____

_____

_____

What compliments do people give me that I find hard to accept?

_____

_____

_____

_____

_____

_____

_____

How can I adjust my thinking to make it easier to not only receive these compliments but believe them?

_____

_____

_____

_____

_____

_____

_____

_____

_____

How I see myself. A self portrait:

What does this picture tell me about how I see myself?

_____

_____

_____

_____

_____

Your mind believes what
you tell it. Feed your
mind with faith,
strength, truth, and love.

These are a few pictures of me I like:
(Paste or staple them below.)

Who is the person I love most in this world? Why?

What could I do to let someone know I love them if I were unable to speak?

Who is the person I admire most in the world? Why?

When you are freely
giving love to others,
don't forget to
give some love
to yourself.

Art from Emotion
Let's find out what my emotions look like as art.

Select a colour to represent each emotion listed below. Start by assigning a colour to the right of each emotion, creating your own colour/emotion legend.

Accomplished	Angry
Calm	Confident
Determined	Disappointed
Excited	Fearful
Happy	Joyful
Loved	Optimistic
Peaceful	Relieved
Sorrow	Surprised
Thankful	Worried

Each day, colour a space in the art on the opposite page with the colour that represents your most predominate emotion that day. Repeat until the art piece is complete.

Emotion
is what
makes art
beautiful.

Art Reflection

Based on the colours in my art piece, which emotion did I experience the most often?

_____

Which emotion did I experience the least?

_____

Did this surprise me? If so, why or why not?

_____

_____

_____

_____

_____

_____

_____

_____

_____

_____

A Positive Life

One of the ways to live a more positive life is to convert negative thoughts or emotions into positive ones.

(Use this page to record some of your own examples.)

Here is an exercise in positivity to try:

Whenever a negative thought enters my mind, I will immediately say or think to myself: "That is not my reality" and replace that negative thought with: "I am so fortunate and thankful for _____."

Chapter

Five

Dreams & Goals

What does a goal of gender equality look like to me?

When you dream,
why not reach for the moon?
Even if you fall short, you will
still land among the stars.

I Have a Dream...
A beautiful dream...

I dream…

_____

_____

_____

_____

_____

_____

_____

_____

_____

_____

_____

_____

_____

_____

_____

_____

_____

Here's the most vivid dream I've had and what I think it means:

_____

_____

_____

_____

_____

_____

_____

_____

_____

_____

_____

_____

_____

_____

_____

_____

_____

_____

_____

Goals are Dreams with a Plan

Here's a list of some of my goals for the coming year:

If I knew I couldn't fail, what would I do?

A list of at least ten things I'd like to accomplish in my lifetime:

_____

_____

_____

_____

_____

_____

_____

_____

_____

_____

_____

_____

_____

_____

_____

_____

_____

_____

_____

_____

If I had a magic key, what would it open? What would be inside?

_____

_____

_____

_____

_____

_____

_____

_____

_____

My dream vacation:

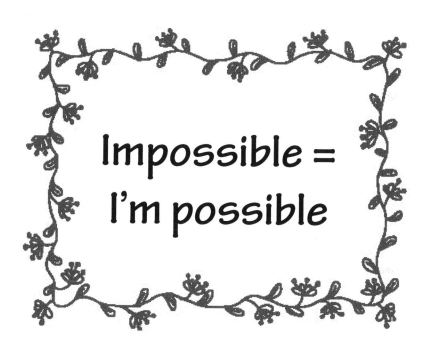

Impossible =
I'm possible

Think about that the next time you believe
something is unattainable for you.

What am I saving for?

Whether it's a new book or an entire new wardrobe,
there is always something worth saving for.

Use this jar to track your savings and reach your goal.
Begin colouring from the bottom up, and
when the jar is full, your goal is reached.

I'm Saving For _____

My $ Goal is _____

Date $ added	Amount added	Running total

If I won $100,000, what would I do with it?

Chapter

Six

Strength & Wisdom

Being Brave

A list of the ways I stay brave and ward off fear:

Don't be afraid to let your inner lion roar.

The bravest person I know is...

Wisdom

With each day, week, month, and year that passes, I gain wisdom.
I am already much wiser than I used to be. If I could go back between five
and ten years, what advice would I give to my younger self?

I am strong when I understand my weaknesses.

My weaknesses are...

_____

_____

_____

_____

_____

_____

_____

_____

_____

_____

_____

_____

_____

_____

_____

_____

I remember a difficult time in my life when...

The harder
I fall, the
higher I will
bounce back.

The Not-So-Bright Spots
and what they've taught me...

Sometimes, life sucks, but there's usually a lesson in there somewhere. What have I learned from the not-so-bright times in my life so far?

_____

_____

_____

_____

_____

_____

_____

_____

_____

_____

_____

_____

_____

_____

_____

_____

_____

_____

Remember a time I fought for something I believed in. How did that experience make me feel?

If someone younger than myself was looking to me for wisdom, what life lessons would I share with them?

When we are wise, we recognize that some people are good for us and others are not.

Who should I be spending more time with? Why?

_____

_____

_____

_____

_____

_____

_____

Who should I be spending less time with? Why?

_____

_____

_____

_____

_____

_____

Chapter

Seven

Health

Keeping a Healthy Mind

A negative mind will never give me a positive life.

We can only attain what our mind believes we can attain.
Changing my mind can change my life.

What do I believe about myself today?

_____

_____

_____

_____

_____

_____

_____

_____

_____

_____

_____

_____

_____

_____

_____

I'm not average. I'm awesome!

Improving My Mind, Body and Soul

What could I work on that would help me to improve my overall health?

_____

_____

_____

_____

_____

_____

_____

_____

_____

_____

What positive things do I already do that help me maintain good health?

_____

_____

_____

_____

_____

_____

_____

_____

My Go-to List
Help and inspiration when needed

Friends I can call on:

_____

_____

_____

_____

_____

_____

Websites:

_____

_____

_____

_____

_____

_____

Help Lines:

_____

_____

_____

_____

Places to go for inspiration:

_____

_____

_____

_____

_____

_____

_____

Other important resources:

_____

_____

_____

_____

_____

_____

_____

I am as unique as my health journey -
and I will not compare myself to others.

Transgender health is a very personal experience. What expectations do I have (or had in the past) about my own health journey?

_____

_____

_____

_____

_____

_____

_____

_____

_____

_____

_____

_____

_____

_____

_____

_____

_____

On the next few pages there are areas that may not apply to you. Use whatever you'd like and leave out the rest.

While you did not choose to be transgender, you do have choices when it comes to your healthcare, including the professionals you may decide to work with along the way. This is an individual journey, and there are no right or wrong answers. You may decide to use the Notes areas to express your own ideas around things like blockers, hormones and surgeries.

My Medical Team:

General Practitioner (AKA family doctor): _____

Address: _____

Phone Number: _____

Notes:

_____

_____

_____

_____

Secondary Practitioner: _____

Address: _____

Phone Number: _____

Notes:

_____

_____

_____

_____

Endocrinologist: _____

Address: _____

Phone Number: _____

Notes:

_____

_____

_____

_____

Therapist: _____

Address: _____

Phone Number: _____

Notes:

_____

_____

_____

_____

Surgeon (if applicable): _____

Address: _____

Phone Number: _____

Notes:

_____

_____

_____

_____

Surgeon (if applicable): _____

Address: _____

Phone Number: _____

Notes:

_____

_____

_____

_____

Surgery Dates (if applicable):

Extra Notes

My Medications & Doses:
(Including Hormone Replacement Therapy if applicable)

Name & Rx #: _____

Dose: _____

First Started on: _____ Ended on: _____

Notes: _____

Name & Rx #: _____

Dose: _____

First Started on: _____ Ended on: _____

Notes: _____

Name & Rx #: _____

Dose: _____

First Started on: _____ Ended on: _____

Notes: _____

Name & Rx #: _____

Dose: _____

First Started on: _____ Ended on: _____

Notes: _____

Name & Rx #: _____

Dose: _____

First Started on: _____ Ended on: _____

Notes: _____

My Transition:

Memories of Important Milestones

The Space Between Genders and What it Has Taught Me:

Chapter

Eight

More Great Stuff

Fun Fact:

It was on purpose that there are eight chapters in this journal.

Spiritually, the number eight is a personal power number that
represents inner wisdom, self-confidence, and truth.
It represents a life path with balance, harmony, strength, and meaning.

The number eight has no beginning and no end. On its side, it is the
mathematical symbol for infinity. It represents endless
abundance in love, supply, time, and energy.

The number eight is also the atomic number for oxygen,
which is pretty important to us as humans.

Just for fun – can you make it through this maze?

This maze represents the many twists and turns in life. A straight line may be easier, but makes for a very boring journey. Your individual experiences, planned or not, make you who you are. The more you experience the twists and turns in life, the richer your life will be.

Enjoy the journey.

What are the best things about living in the world today?

_____

_____

_____

_____

_____

_____

_____

_____

What are the worst things about living in the world today?

_____

_____

_____

_____

_____

_____

_____

_____

One person can make a difference.

What can I do to make the world a better place?

A list of the things I should try to do more often:

A little about my favourite movies or TV shows that feature a transgender person and why I like them:

_____

_____

_____

_____

_____

_____

_____

_____

_____

_____

_____

_____

_____

_____

_____

_____

_____

If I could sit on a bench and talk for an hour with anyone, past or living, who would it be? What would I want to talk about?

Life is An Adventure

Life may not always turn out the way we expect but that doesn't
mean the journey you are on is not the one you were meant to take.

What if we are all spiritual beings here to learn from what this world
can teach us? In the school of life, there are no wrong lessons. Sure,
some are tougher than others to master and some near impossible, but
each lesson is invaluable. You succeed in life not when you master everything,
but when you decide to try, to step up and be the best
person you can be in the time you are here.

Remember to rejoice in life because even in the most trying
times, you are learning, growing, and expanding as the
unique and wonderful being that you are.

I am here for a reason. I am wonderfully
and purposely made - and I am enough!

Don't let
anyone steal
your sparkle.

Fun Facts:

The first rainbow flag was created as a symbol of pride and hope for the LGBT (lesbian, gay, bisexual and transgender) community in 1978. It was designed and stitched together by Gilbert Baker Designs. Harvey Milk is credited for providing the inspiration.

The transgender flag was created in 1999, and while numerous variations of the design exist today, it was originally created by a transgender woman by the name of Monica Helms. This is what Helms said about her design: "The stripes at the top and bottom are light blue, the traditional color for baby boys. The stripes next to them are pink, the traditional color for baby girls. The stripe in the middle is white, for those who are intersex, transitioning, or consider themselves having a neutral or undefined gender. The pattern is such that no matter which way you fly it, it is always correct, signifying us finding correctness in our lives."

There are over 700,000 people who identify as transgender, and that is just in the United States, let alone the rest of the world. That is no small number! You are not alone. As a transgender individual, you have the unique privilege of viewing the world in a way most people will never get to experience. That makes you pretty special.

Five Fun Facts About Me:

1. _____
   _____
   _____

2. _____
   _____
   _____

3. _____
   _____
   _____

4. _____
   _____
   _____

5. _____
   _____
   _____

A strong person
always has scars.
Be proud of yours.

A Page Dedicated to My Doodles 😊
Just Because...

Final Notes & Other Random Stuff:

_____

_____

_____

_____

_____

_____

_____

_____

_____

_____

_____

_____

_____

_____

_____

This journal may be complete, but your story is not. Keep journaling and recording all the experiences and lessons life offers you. One day, you may decide to share your story with the world, and this journal can serve as a piece of your history to help you do just that.

I Finished This Journal:

/   /

Made in the USA
San Bernardino, CA
12 June 2019